P9-BZE-760

J 796.3 KENNEDY

Kennedy, Mike,

Meet the Patriots

HUDSON PUBLIC LIBRARY
3 WASHINGTON ST
@WOOD SQUARE
HUDSON, MA 01749

DISCARD

SMART ABOUT SPORTS

Meet the Patriots

By
Mike Kennedy
with Mark Stewart

NORWOOD HOUSE PRESS

SEP 20 2010

DISCARD

Norwood House Press, P.O. Box 316598, Chicago, Illinois 60631

For information regarding Norwood House Press,
please visit our website at: www.norwoodhousepress.com or call 866-565-2900.

Photo Credits:
  Associated Press (4), Black Book Partners (7, 15), Getty Images (8, 12, 13, 16, 18, 20, 21, 22, 23).
Cover Photos:
  Top Left: Topps, Inc.; Top Right: James D. Smith/Icon SMI; Bottom Left: Rhona Wise/Icon SMI;
  Bottom Right: Fleer Corp.
The football memorabilia photographed for this book is part of the authors' collection:
  Page 6) Drew Bledsoe: Action Packed, Inc., Page 10) Gino Cappelletti: Fleer Corp.;
  Jim Nance, Steve Grogan & John Hannah: Topps, Inc., Page 11) Mike Haynes: Topps, Inc.; Ty Law: Fleer Corp.;
  Tom Brady: Score, Inc.; Tedy Bruschi: TIME Inc./Sports Illustrated for Kids.
Special thanks to Topps, Inc.

Editor: Brian Fitzgerald
Designer: Ron Jaffe
Project Management: Black Book Partners, LLC.
Editorial Production: Jessica McCulloch

HUDSON PUBLIC LIBRARY
WOOD SQUARE
HUDSON, MA 01749

LIBRARY OF CONGRESS CATALOGING-IN-PUBLICATION DATA
     Kennedy, Mike, 1965-
       Meet the Patriots / by Mike Kennedy with Mark Stewart.
          p. cm.
       Includes bibliographical references and index.
       Summary: "An introductory look at the New England Patriots football team.
     Includes a brief history, facts, photos, records, glossary, and fun
     activities"--Provided by publisher.
       ISBN-13: 978-1-59953-396-4 (library edition : alk. paper)
       ISBN-10: 1-59953-396-0 (library edition : alk. paper)
       1. New England Patriots (Football team)--History--Juvenile literature. I.
     Stewart, Mark, 1960- II. Title.
       GV956.N36K46 2010
       796.332'640974461--dc22
                         2010007369

© 2011 by Norwood House Press. All rights reserved.
No part of this book may be reproduced without written permission from the publisher.
The New England Patriots is a registered trademark of New England Patriots L.P.
This publication is not affiliated with the New England Patriots, New England Patriots L.P.,
The National Football League, or The National Football League Players Association.

Manufactured in the United States of America in North Mankato, Minnesota.
156N–072010

Contents

Words in **bold type** are defined on page 24.

Victory! The Patriots are champions for the first time.

The New England Patriots

Sports fans in New England like their teams to play hard. That is no problem for the Patriots. They never give up. The Patriots know what it takes to win.

Once Upon a Time

The Patriots played their first season in 1960. They later became one of the best teams in the National Football

League (NFL). The Patriots have always put great players on the field. Drew Bledsoe and Tom Brady were two of the best.

Tom Brady practices hard before each game.

Fans watch a game at Gillette Stadium.

At the Stadium

The Patriots play their home
games at Gillette Stadium.
It was built in 2002. Fans
have fun inside and outside
the stadium. It includes a
bridge and a lighthouse.

Shoe Box

The cards on these pages belong to the authors. They show some of the best Patriots ever.

Gino Cappelletti

Kicker/Receiver
• 1960–1970
Gino Cappelletti caught passes and kicked for the team.

Jim Nance

Running Back
• 1965–1971
Tackling big Jim Nance was not easy. It was like trying to stop a train.

John Hannah

Offensive Lineman
• 1973–1985
John Hannah made the **Pro Bowl** nine times.

John Hannah

Steve Grogan

Quarterback
• 1975–1990
Steve Grogan was a good passer and runner.

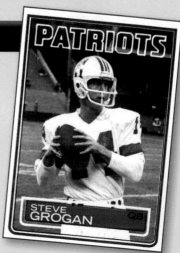

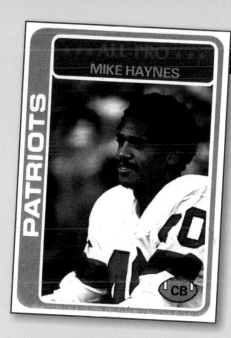

Mike Haynes

Defensive Back
• 1976–1982
Mike Haynes stuck
to his man like glue.

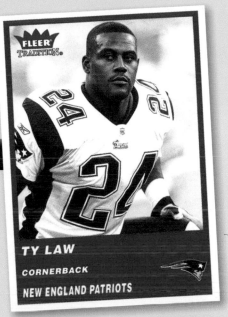

Ty Law

Defensive Back
• 1995–2004
Ty Law played
his best in the
big games.

Tedy Bruschi

Linebacker • 1996–2008
The Patriots played
extra hard when
Tedy Bruschi was
on the field.

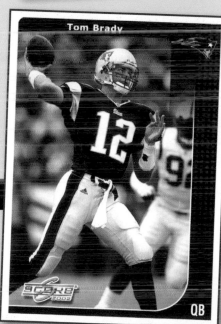

Tom Brady

Quarterback • 2000–
Tom Brady led
the team to three
Super Bowl wins.

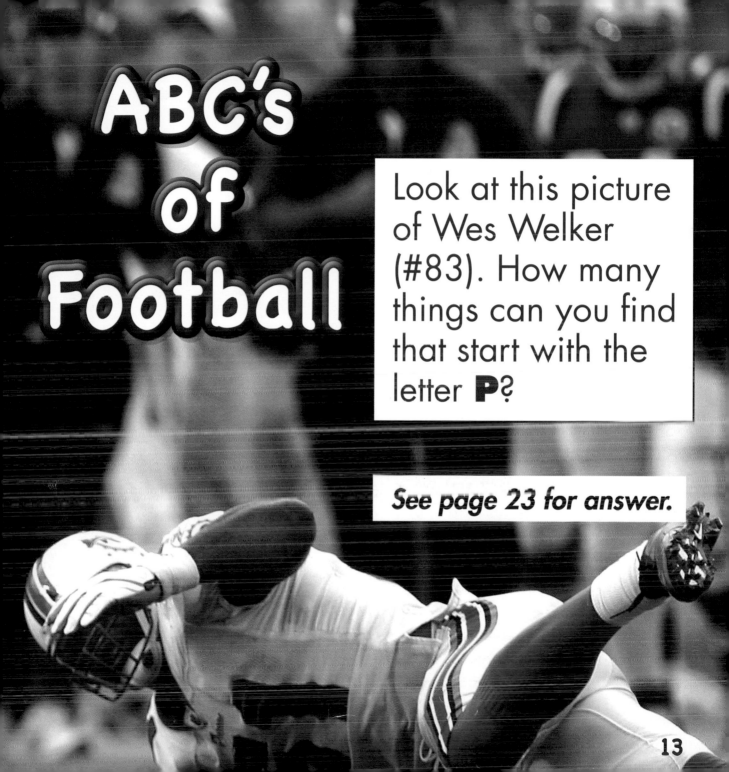

ABC's of Football

Look at this picture of Wes Welker (#83). How many things can you find that start with the letter **P**?

See page 23 for answer.

Brain Games

Here is a poem about a famous Patriot:

There once was a passer named Drew.
He starred in the silver and blue.
When he dropped back to throw,
He put on a show.
There was nothing the defense could do.

Guess which one of these facts is **TRUE**:

- *Drew Bledsoe led the Patriots to the Super Bowl.*

- *Drew stood 5 feet, 5 inches tall.*

See page 23 for answer.

Drew Bledsoe warms up before a game.

Pat Patriot leads the charge!

Fun on the Field

Pat Patriot is the team's mascot. He wears a team uniform and a hat with stars on it. The fans love Pat. He leads the players onto the field before every home game.

On the Map

The Patriots call Foxboro, Massachusetts home. The players come from all over the world. These Patriots played in the Pro Bowl. Match each with the place he was born:

1 **Babe Parilli • Pro Bowl: 1963–1964 & 1966**
Rochester, Pennsylvania

2 **Russ Francis • Pro Bowl: 1976–1978**
Seattle, Washington

3 **Stanley Morgan • Pro Bowl: 1979–1980 & 1986–1987**
Easley, South Carolina

4 **Mosi Tatupu • Pro Bowl: 1986**
Pago Pago, American Samoa

5 **Willie McGinest**
• Pro Bowl: 1996 & 2003
Long Beach, California

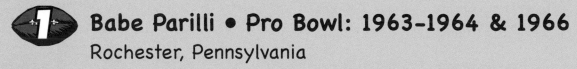

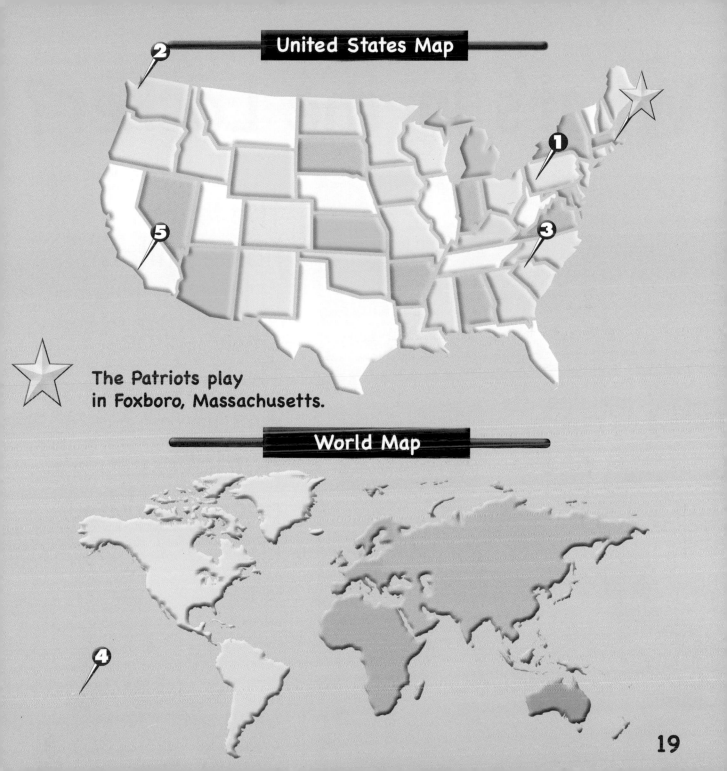

United States Map

The Patriots play
in Foxboro, Massachusetts.

World Map

What's in the Locker?

The team's home uniform is blue. It has silver stripes. There is a picture of a patriot on each shoulder.

Jerod Mayo wears the team's home uniform.

The team's road uniform is white. It has blue stripes. The team usually wears a silver helmet. It has a picture of a patriot on each side.

Randy Moss wears the team's road uniform.

We Won!

From 2002 to 2005, the Patriots won the Super Bowl three times. Their first win may have been the best game of all. They made the winning kick with no time left.

Adam Vinatieri jumps in the air after his game-winning kick.

Record Book

These Patriots stars set team records.

Running Back	Record	Year
Curtis Martin*	14 **touchdowns**	1995
Corey Dillon	1,635 **yards**	2004

* Martin also had 14 touchdowns in 1996.

Quarterback/Receiver	Record	Year
Tom Brady	50 touchdown passes	2007
Randy Moss	23 touchdown catches	2007
Wes Welker	123 catches	2009

Answer for ABC's of Football
*Here are some words in the picture that start with **P**: Pad, Pants, Patriots Uniform.*
Did you find any others?

Answer for Brain Games
The first fact is true. The Patriots played in the Super Bowl in 1997. Drew Bledsoe was their quarterback. He stood 6 feet, 5 inches.

Football Words

PRO BOWL
A special game played between the NFL's top stars.

SUPER BOWL
The game that decides the champion of the NFL.

TOUCHDOWNS
Scoring plays worth six points.

YARDS
A yard is a distance of three feet. A football field is 100 yards from goal line to goal line.

Index

Photos are on **bold** numbered pages.

About the Patriots

Learn more about the Patriots at www.patriots.com

Learn more about football at www.profootballhof.com